SHORT WALKS
MADE EASY

DARTMOOR

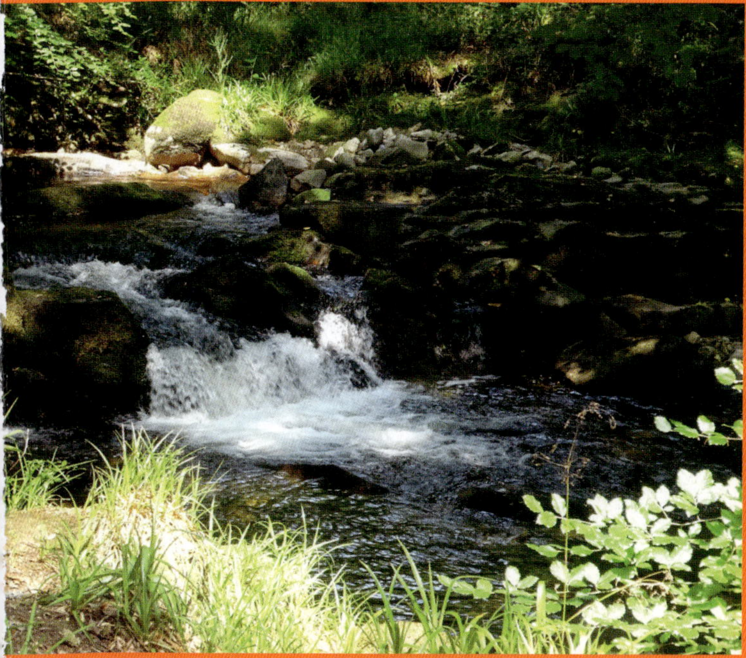

Contents

Getting outside on Dartmoor		6
We smile more when we're outside		8
Respecting the countryside		10
Using this guide		11
Walk 1	Okehampton and Fatherford	**14**
Walk 2	Fingle Woods	**20**
Photos	Scenes from the walks	26
Walk 3	Yarner Wood	**28**
Walk 4	Haytor Quarry and Tramway	**34**
Photos	Wildlife interest	40
Walk 5	Bellever Forest	**42**
Walk 6	Princetown and Fogintor Quarry	**48**
Walk 7	RAF Harrowbeer	**54**
Photos	Cafés and pubs	60
Walk 8	Burrator Arboretum	**62**
Walk 9	Shipley Bridge and the Avon Dam	**68**
Walk 10	Longtimber Woods	**74**
Credits		80

Map symbols	Front cover flap
Accessibility and what to take	Back cover flap
Walk locations	Inside front cover
Your next adventure?	Inside back cover

Walk 1

OKEHAMPTON AND FATHERFORD

Distance
2.8 miles / 4.5km

Time
1½ hours

Start/Finish
Okehampton Station

Parking EX20 1EJ
Okehampton Station car park

Cafés/pubs
The Bulleid Buffet, Okehampton Station

Delightful old tramway path along wooded East Okement River valley

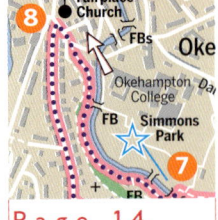

Page 14

Walk 2
FINGLE WOODS

Distance
3.3 miles / 5.3 km

Time
2 hours

Start/Finish
Fingle Bridge

Parking EX6 6PW
By Fingle Bridge

Cafés/pubs
Fingle Bridge Inn

Stunningly wooded Teign Gorge overlooked by craggy Sharp Tor

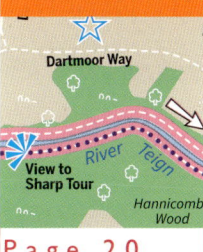

Page 20

Walk 3
YARNER WOOD

Distance
1.7 miles / 2.7 km

Time
1 hour

Start/Finish
Yarner Wood

Parking TQ13 9LJ
Middle Trendlebere car park

Cafés/pubs
Nearest in Bovey Tracey

Lofty beeches, ancient oaks and woodland birds, flowers and fungi

Page 28

Walk 4
HAYTOR QUARRY AND TRAMWAY

Distance
1.8 miles / 2.9 km

Time
1¼ hours *CATCH A BUS*

Start/Finish
Haytor

Parking TQ13 9XT
Dartmoor NP Visitor Centre car park

Cafés/pubs
In Haytor Vale

Moorland stroll on granite tramway with far-reaching tor views

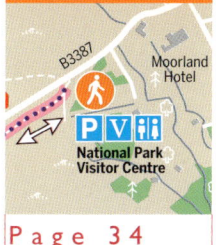

Page 34

Contents 3

Walk 5

BELLEVER FOREST

Distance
2.4 miles/3.8km

Time
1½ hours

Start/Finish
Bellever Forest, Postbridge

Parking PL20 6TU
Forestry England Bellever Forest car park

Cafés/pubs
East Dart Inn, Postbridge

CATCH A BUS

A forest and heathland walk rich in Bronze Age relics, with great views

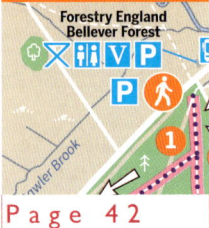

Page 42

Walk 6

PRINCETOWN AND FOGGINTOR QUARRY

Distance
3.7 miles/6km

Time
2 hours

Start/Finish
Princetown

Parking PL20 6QG
Station Road car park

Cafés/pubs
Princetown

CATCH A BUS

Grand vistas and tor views; moorland birds; quarrying heritage

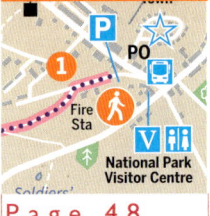

Page 48

Walk 7

RAF HARROWBEER

Distance
2.4 miles/3.8km

Time
1½ hours

Start/Finish
Yelverton

Parking PL20 6DJ
Leg o' Mutton Corner car park

Cafés/pubs
Dartmoor Bakery; Yelverton

CATCH A BUS

An open common walk across a WWII airbase, now grazed by ponies

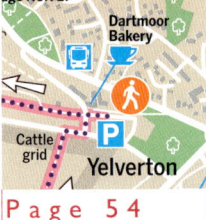

Page 54

4 Short Walks Made Easy

Walk 8
BURRATOR ARBORETUM

Distance
0.7 miles/1.1km

Time
½ hour

Start/Finish
Burrator Arboretum

Parking PL20 6PF
Burrator Arboretum and Nature Reserve car park

Cafés/pubs
Nearest: Royal Oak Inn, Meavy

Glorious arboretum nature trail; pretty brook; wildlife pond

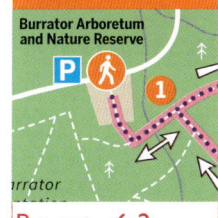

Page 62

Walk 9
SHIPLEY BRIDGE AND THE AVON DAM

Distance
3.7 miles/5.9km

Time
2 hours

Start/Finish
Shipley Bridge

Parking TQ10 9EL
Avon Dam car park

Cafés/pubs
Picnic tables at 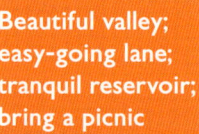, ❹ and ❻

Beautiful valley; easy-going lane; tranquil reservoir; bring a picnic

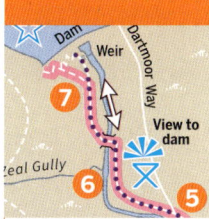

Page 68

Walk 10
LONGTIMBER WOODS

Distance
1.7 miles/2.7km

Time
1 hour *CATCH A BUS*

Start/Finish
Station Road, Ivybridge

Parking PL21 0AG
Roadside on Station Road

Cafés/pubs
Picnic tables at ❸; Ivybridge

Sparkling River Erme; have a riverside picnic; paper-making heritage

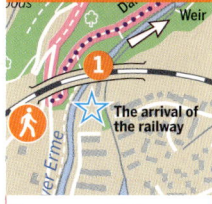

Page 74

Contents 5

GETTING OUTSIDE ON DARTMOOR

" "

Fabulous views of this wild and beautiful tor-studded moorland, so evocative of Conan Doyle's *The Hound of the Baskervilles*

OS Champion
Tom Sigler

Burrator Woods

A very warm welcome to the new Short Walks Made Easy guide to Dartmoor – what a fantastic selection of leisurely walks we have for you!

Dartmoor is part of a vast, raised granite plateau forming the largest area of wild country in southern Britain. It was designated as a national park in 1951 and covers an area of 368 square miles between Okehampton and Ivybridge, north to south, and Tavistock and Bovey Tracey, west to east.

Over millennia, where the granite has been exposed through erosion by rain, wind and frost, giant blocks of stone have been weathered to form tors. Fabulous views of this wild and beautiful tor-studded moorland, so evocative of Conan Doyle's *The Hound of the Baskervilles*, can be seen on the comparatively gentle walks at Haytor and high on the moor from Princetown.

The combination of unyielding granite and high rainfall has given rise to a number of sparkling streams, and the routes to riverside picnic sites along the delightfully pretty Avon and Erme valleys lead you beside two fine examples.

The Dartmoor National Park Authority has implemented a 'Miles Without Stiles' initiative providing accessible routes at various locations around the moor, and five of these form the basis for walks in this guide, including the glorious woodland strolls at Yarner Wood, Bellever Forest and Burrator Arboretum. There's also fascinating wartime history to discover at Harrowbeer and tramway heritage to enjoy at Okehampton.

Tom Sigler,
OS Champion

WE SMILE MORE
WHEN WE'RE OUTSIDE

Near Haytor

Whether it's a short walk during our lunch break or a full day's outdoor adventure, we know that a good dose of fresh air is just the tonic we all need.

At Ordnance Survey (OS), we're passionate about helping more people to get outside more often. It sits at the heart of everything we do, and through our products and services, we aim to help you lead an active outdoor lifestyle, so that you can live longer, stay younger and enjoy life more.

We firmly believe the outdoors is for everyone, and we want to help you find the very best Great Britain has to offer. We are blessed with an island that is beautiful and unique, with a rich and varied landscape. There are coastal paths to meander along, woodlands to explore, countryside to roam, and cities to uncover. Our trusted source of inspirational content is bursting with ideas for places to go, things to do and easy beginner's guides on how to get started.

It can be daunting when you're new to something, so we want to bring you the know-how from the people who live and breathe the outdoors. To help guide us, our team of awe-inspiring OS Champions share their favourite places to visit, hints and tips for outdoor adventures, as well as tried and tested accessible, family- and wheelchair-friendly routes. We hope that you will feel inspired to spend more time outside and reap the physical and mental health benefits that the outdoors has to offer. With our handy guides, paper and digital mapping, and exciting new apps, we can be with you every step of the way.

To find out more visit os.uk/getoutside

RESPECTING THE COUNTRYSIDE

You can't beat getting outside in the British countryside, but it's vital that we leave no trace when we're enjoying the great outdoors.

Let's make sure that generations to come can enjoy the countryside just as we do.

 Leave no trace

 Keep dogs under control; bin and bag waste

 Do not light fires; only BBQ at official sites

 Leave gates as you find them

 Keep to footpaths and open access land

 Plan ahead for your trip

For more details please visit www.gov.uk/countryside-code

USING THIS GUIDE

Easy-to-follow Dartmoor walks for all

Before setting off

Check the walk information panel to plan your outing
- Consider using **Public transport** where flagged. If driving, note the satnav postcode for the car park under **Parking**
- The suggested **Time** is based on a gentle pace
- Note the availability of **Cafés**, tearooms and pubs, and **Toilets**

Terrain and hilliness
- **Terrain** indicates the nature of the route surface
- Any rises and falls are noted under **Hilliness**

Walking with your dog?
- This panel states where **Dogs** must be on a lead and how many stiles there are – in case you need to lift your dog
- Keep dogs on leads where there are livestock and between April and August in forest and on grassland where there are ground-nesting birds

A perfectly pocket-sized walking guide
- Handily sized for ease of use on each walk
- When not being read, it fits nicely into a pocket...
- ...so between points, put this book in the pocket of your coat, trousers or day sack and enjoy your stroll in glorious countryside – we've made it pocket-sized for a reason!

Flexibility of route presentation to suit all readers
- **Not comfortable map reading?** Then use the simple-to-follow route profile and accompanying route description and pictures
- **Happy to map read?** New-look walk mapping makes it easier for you to focus on the route and the points of interest along the way
- **Read the insightful Did you know?, Local legend, Stories behind the walk** and **Nature notes** to help you make the most of your day out and to enjoy all that each walk has to offer

OS information about the walk

- Many of the features and symbols shown are taken from Ordnance Survey's celebrated **Explorer** mapping, designed to help people across Great Britain enjoy leisure time spent outside

- National Grid reference for the start point
- Explorer sheet map covering the route

OS information
SX 591944
Explorer OL28

The easy-to-use walk map

- **Large-scale** mapping for ultra-clear route finding

- **Numbered points** at key turns along the route that tie in with the route instructions and respective points marked on the profile

- **Pictorial symbols** for intuitive map reading, see Map Symbols on the front cover flap

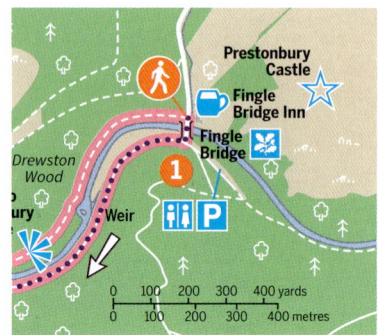

The simple-to-follow walk profile

- Progress easily along the route using the illustrative profile, it has **numbered points** for key turning points and **graduated distance** markers

- Easy-read **route directions** with turn-by-turn detail

- Reassuring **route photographs** for each numbered point

12 · Short Walks Made Easy

Using QR codes

- Scan each QR code to see the route in Ordnance Survey's OS Maps App
NB You may need to download a scanning app if you have an older phone

- OS Maps will open the route automatically if you have it installed. If not, the route will open in the web version of OS Maps

- Please click **Start Route** button to begin navigating or **Download Route** to store the route for offline use

WALK 1

OKEHAMPTON AND FATHERFORD

Okehampton Station opened in 1871 under the Devon & Cornwall Railway Company, which was absorbed into the London & South Western Railway in 1872. The walk starts along an old horse-drawn tramway (1870s to 1930s), used to carry slate and stone from quarries at Fatherford and Halstock. Near Tramlines Wood is the coach house and stables, where wagons and horses were kept. The walk encounters the lofty railway viaduct, built in 1870, and then returns alongside the East Okement River.

OS information
SX 591944
Explorer OL28

Distance
2.8 miles/4.5km

Time
1½ hours

Start/Finish
Okehampton Station

Parking EX20 1EJ
Okehampton Station car park

Public toilets
St James Street, Okehampton

Cafés/pubs
The Bulleid Buffet, Okehampton Station

Terrain
Well-surfaced track ❶ to ❹, woodland and recreation ground paths; pavement

Hilliness
Level or gently descending, with steady ascent from ❽ to end

Footwear
Year round

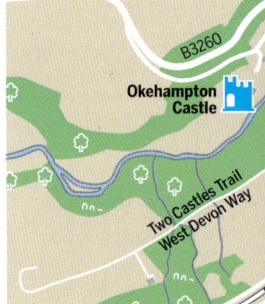

Public transport

Rail services via Exeter and Crediton: travelinesw.com. Bus services to 🚶 from Exeter, Tavistock and Launceston: stagecoachbus.com; gocornwallbus.co.uk

Accessibility

Powered chairs 🚶 to ④ and ⑦ (Simmons Park) to end; all-terrain pushchairs throughout

Dogs

Welcome but keep on leads in Simmons Park and in town. No stiles

Did you know? Regular passenger railway services to and from Okehampton ended in 1972, although trains serviced Meldon Quarry until 2005. The Dartmoor Line – the first railway to be brought back into full passenger service under the Government's Restoring Your Railway initiative – was officially re-opened in November 2021 after several years of operation as a heritage line. Regular services now run to Exeter via Crediton; more than 250,000 people travelled on the railway during its first year of operation.

Local legend Fitz's Well and Cross can be found on the edge of East Hill above Okehampton. The story tells of a man and his wife who got lost on the moor (fog-bound and tricked by pixies). On coming across the well, they took a drink: the pixies' spell was broken and the fog lifted. The cross is said to have been erected in thanksgiving and as a marker to help others in a similar plight.

Walk 1 Okehampton and Fatherford

STORIES BEHIND THE WALK

Okehampton Castle This is the largest castle in Devon. It was built by Baldwin de Brionne soon after the Norman Conquest in 1066, and guards a crossing point of the West Okement River. Much of what remains of the motte-and-bailey structure dates from the 13th and 15th centuries. It was set within an extensive deer park and converted to a sumptuous residence in the 14th century by Hugh Courtenay, Earl of Devon, but fell into ruin after the Courtenays fell out with Henry VIII in 1539 (english-heritage.org.uk).

Sydney Simmons Born in a humble cottage in 1840, Sydney Simmons became Okehampton's greatest benefactor. He moved to London and invented an automatic carpet beater; he became extremely wealthy but never forgot his roots. He built almshouses around the town and, when the council wanted to build houses alongside the East Okement River, he bought the land and paid for landscaping and its ongoing maintenance. In 1906, the area became Simmons Park, gifted to the town for locals to enjoy.

The Granite Way — Tramlines Bridleway — Tramlines Wood — Tramlines Bridleway — ½ mile

Station car park

- From the station car park, walk **down** the access road to the junction.
- Turn **right** onto Station Road to reach the first turning on the right in 25 yards.

1 ➤ Signed Tramlines bridleway, go **right** on the old tramway, passing houses to reach a large wooden gate.

2 ➤ Pass through the gate into the Woodland Trust's Tramlines Wood and follow the track high above the East Okement River for almost ½ mile to a gate.

16 Short Walks Made Easy

☆ The Army on Dartmoor and Ten Tors

Okehampton Camp, on the edge of the moor above the town, was built in 1893, 20 years after the military started using parts of the moor for training purposes. The camp hosts the annual Ten Tors Challenge, held in May, which sees 2,400 teenagers undertake a strenuous walking and camping expedition on the moor. There are three military ranges on Dartmoor: Okehampton, Merrivale and Willsworthy.

☆ The Granite Way

The Granite Way is an 11-mile multi-use route that utilises the trackbed of the old London & South Western Railway line, extended from Okehampton to Lydford in 1874. West of Okehampton the line crosses the valley of the West Okement River via the impressive Meldon Viaduct, which towers 150 feet above the river, then rounds the north-west corner of Dartmoor to pass the village of Sourton and its lovely Grade II-listed church.

Tramlines Bridleway — ④ — Viaduct — ⑤ — 1 mile — Ball Hill Conservation Area

③ ▪ Exit the wood and descend gently on a surfaced track across an open grassy area.
▪ Re-enter woodland and pass a house; go through the gate by a ford and under the railway viaduct to a path junction.

④ ▪ Turn **left** over the bridge; go under the viaduct and pass the ford.
▪ Go through a gate, and then head up the lane to a parking area.

Walk 1 Okehampton and Fatherford

NATURE NOTES

The moorland slopes around Okehampton – a mix of old oak woodland and open ground, once part of Okehampton Castle's medieval deer park – are renowned for their display of bluebells in May, preceded in some spots by pungent wild garlic (ramsons). Despite their beauty and heady scent, bluebells are poisonous to humans, dogs, cattle and horses.

In spring look out for delicate white wood anemone and wood sorrel: the latter has distinctive trefoil leaves and in the past was used to treat scurvy on account of its high vitamin C content.

The gardens and woodland of Simmons Park attract the gregarious and distinctive long-tailed tit, usually in close-knit groups, calling in thin, high-pitched calls to keep in contact as they search the trees for small insects.

From spring through to autumn, speckled wood butterflies may be seen along the old tramway, preferring the dappled sunlight of the tree-lined track.

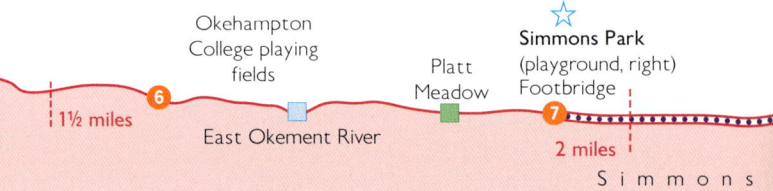

5 ➤ At the end of the parking area turn **left** through a gate into Ball Hill Conservation Area.
➤ Follow the path for ½ mile to a gate at the woodland edge.
➤ Exit the wood to the junction of tracks ahead. Bear slightly **left** on a narrow path that passes a ford to reach a bridge.

6 ➤ **Cross** Kempley Bridge into Okehampton College playing fields.
➤ Head towards the river then turn **right**, under trees, beside it.
➤ Pass a bridge and continue through Platt Meadow to reach Simmons Park (playground, right).

18 Short Walks Made Easy

Above: long-tailed tit
Below: wild garlic (left), bluebells (right)

Top: speckled wood butterfly
Above: wood anemone

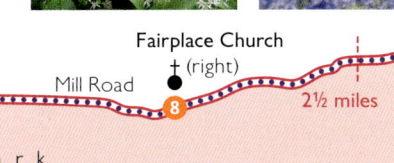

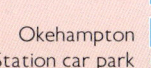

(7) ▶ Go **left** over the bridge then **right** on a tarmac path that parallels the river for ⅓ mile, passing Swiss Cottage to the park's ornamental gates.
▶ Keep **forward** onto Mill Road and in 50 yards reach Station Road on the left (Fairplace Church, right).

(8) ▶ Turn **left** up Station Road, ascending steadily.
▶ In ⅓ mile, take the first road **left** (Station Road – Victorian drinking fountain at the junction) to return to the station access road.

WALK 2

FINGLE WOODS

Following an impressive wooded gorge cut by the River Teign, this very pretty walk passes through one of the river's loveliest sections: beautiful oak and beech trees crowd the riverbanks; dippers and wagtails flit between boulders in the water; salmon and sea trout head upstream to spawn. This riverside ramble offers two options from 17th-century Fingle Bridge: a there-and-back route along the south bank 🚶 to ❺ (wheelchair accessible to ❸), and a circuit with a more challenging return along the north bank.

OS information
SX 743899 Explorer OL28
Distance 3.3 miles/5.3km
Time 2 hours
Start/Finish Fingle Bridge, ¾ mile south-east of Drewsteignton
Parking EX6 6PW Laneside parking areas before Fingle Bridge Inn (accessing parking area on south side of Fingle Bridge is *very* narrow)
Public toilets Fingle Bridge (south side parking area)
Cafés/pubs Fingle Bridge Inn

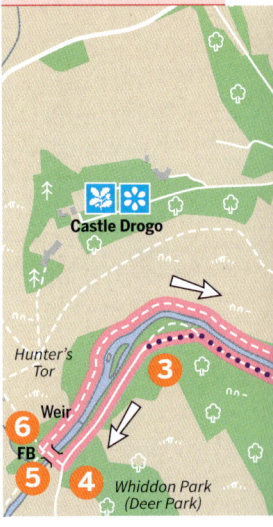

20   Short Walks Made Easy

Terrain
① to ③ – woodland track, stony and rough in places; ③ to end – rougher path with rocky sections

Hilliness
Mostly gentle ascents and descents following the contours of the gorge, but with big steps at ⑦

Footwear
Winter 🥾
Spring/Summer/Autumn 👟 to ⑤
⑥ to end – 🥾

Public transport
None (nearest bus stop at Drewsteignton, with services to Exeter, Okehampton and Moretonhampstead: stagecoachbus.com)

Accessibility
Powered wheelchairs, 👟 to ③; all-terrain pushchairs to the bridge at ⑤

Dogs
Welcome but keep on leads between 1 March and 31 July (lambing/ground bird-nesting season). One (stone) stile

Did you know? Fingle Woods (eight different woodlands) is owned and managed by the Woodland Trust and National Trust in partnership. For centuries the woodlands hosted a flourishing charcoal industry, which ceased after World War II. Castle Drogo, located in a commanding position overlooking the wooded gorge, had its own electricity supply between 1927 and 1994 – the hydro turbine on the River Teign, just before ③, was restored in 2017 and now serves the visitor centre there.

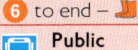

Walk 2 Fingle Woods 21

STORIES BEHIND THE WALK

🌼 Castle Drogo and the Drewes
Castle Drogo, a family home built between 1911 and 1930 (construction was halted during World War I), is renowned as the last 'castle' to be built in England. Self-made millionaire Julius Drewe established his family seat here because he mistakenly believed that his ancestors had connections with the nearby village of Drewsteignton. He commissioned the architect Sir Edwin Lutyens to design a comfortable 20th-century home, but with all the grandeur of a medieval castle (nationaltrust.org.uk).

☆ Teign Valley hillforts
On the return leg of the walk, after climbing the steps at ⑦, look ahead to spot a large and very steep-sided hill rising above Fingle Bridge. On the summit, earthworks denote the ramparts of Prestonbury Castle, one of three Iron Age hillforts that overlook the Teign Gorge. The others, both on the south side of the gorge, are Cranbrook Castle (½ mile to the south) and Wooston Castle (1¼ miles to the east).

☕ Fingle Bridge Inn — weir — Hannicombe Wood

🚶 ① — River Teign — ½ mile

Laneside parking

🌼 **Fingle Bridge**

🅿️ (south side of bridge)

🚻

▶ From the entrance to Fingle Bridge Inn, **cross** Fingle Bridge to a path junction and information board on the far side.

① ▶ Turn **right** along a broad track through Hannicombe Wood, continuing upstream for 1 mile to a path junction/three-way fingerpost. (Pass a weir then walk below a conifer plantation; spot the craggy outline of Sharp Tor high on the gorge's north side.)

22 Short Walks Made Easy

🦋 Fingle Bridge

Fingle Bridge is an old packhorse bridge, thought to date from the 17th century. The Fingle Bridge Inn, a popular watering hole by the bridge, occupies the same site as Jessie Ashplant's tea shelter, founded in 1897 to serve the needs of fishermen, tourists and people delivering grain to Fingle Mill. The mill, which burned down in 1894, stood downriver on the south bank; sections of the leat that used to supply the mill from the weir can still be found.

☆ Long-distance walking routes

Fingle Bridge has long been an important crossing point of the River Teign, and today is utilised by the Dartmoor Way, a 108-mile circular walking route around the edge of the moor. The Dartmoor Way crosses the bridge then follows the Hunters Path along the northern rim of the Teign Gorge, a stretch shared with the Two Moors Way/Devon Coast to Coast (117 miles). Both routes encounter Sharp Tor, glimpsed through the trees on the approach to ②.

②
- At the junction, ignore the Deer Stalkers Path and keep **straight on** to a fork in 400 yards.
- Keep **left** at the fork, passing above Castle Drogo's hydro turbine. Walk to a gate in the granite wall enclosing Whiddon Deer Park in 150 yards.

③
- Pass through the gate and follow the track alongside a wall.
- In 400 yards, look out for a stone stile and footpath signpost on the right.

Walk 2 Fingle Woods

NATURE NOTES

The Upper Teign river is one of Dartmoor's salmon, brown trout and sea trout fishing hotspots. In October and November, salmon can be seen leaping up the fish pass by the weir below Castle Drogo when they return to their birthplace to spawn (and then usually die), after an astonishingly long journey across the Atlantic.

The mixed habitats in Fingle Woods support a diverse range of flora and fauna. Thirty-six species of breeding birds have been recorded; there are otters along the river, fallow deer and hazel dormice in the woodlands, 12 bat species and a number of rare butterflies, such as dingy skippers and pearl-bordered fritillaries.

Low-growing whortleberry – its edible fruit known as 'whorts' – fringes the path; look out, too, for an impressive wood ant nest.

A wealth of mosses and lichens drape around damp boulders and tree branches: the most easily identified is *Usnea articulata*, 'string of sausages' lichen.

In spring delicate wild daffodils adorn the riverbank.

Brown trout

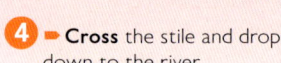

4 ▸ **Cross** the stile and drop down to the river.

5 ▸ **Cross** the river on the Iron Bridge and then ascend steps to reach a path on the north bank.

Wild daffodils, River Teign

Top: whortleberry
Middle: mossy boulder
Bottom: string of sausages lichen

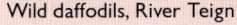

View to Prestonbury Castle (hill fort)

2½ miles

3 miles

Drewston Wood

Laneside parking; Fingle Bridge Inn

Fingle Bridge (right)

(right, on south side of bridge)

6 ▶ Turn **right** (downstream) to pass the weir and the salmon leap, and later the hydro turbine on the opposite bank.

▶ Continue on the rough path through pretty deciduous woodland to steps at the base of Sharp Tor.

7 ▶ Ascend the steep, rocky steps – there's a rail to assist you in places. The descent is easier.

▶ Continue downstream on the rough path for just over 1 mile through Drewston Wood, negotiating steps in places, to reach Fingle Bridge.

Walk 2 Fingle Woods

This page (clockwise): view north from Haytor; Bowerman's Nose, Hound Tor; Fitz's Well and Cross, Okehampton; River Teign, Fingle Woods

Opposite (clockwise): Treneman's Pool, River Erme; Templer Way marker, Haytor Quarry; 'Conchies Road', Princetown

WALK 3

YARNER WOOD

Yarner Wood, near Bovey Tracey, is one of three woodland areas that make up the East Dartmoor Woods and Heaths National Nature Reserve. Dartmoor National Park Authority has set up a 'Miles Without Stiles' route through these beautiful sessile oak woodlands, utilising compacted gravel tracks. Expect steady ascents and descents, and some rough and stony ground. Give yourself time to stop in one of the three hides along the way: Yarner Wood is home to a fantastic range of birds.

OS information
SX 782792 Explorer OL28
Distance 1.7 miles/2.7km
Time 1 hour
Start/Finish Yarner Wood
Parking TQ13 9LJ Middle Trendlebere car park, 2 miles west of Bovey Tracey
Public toilets At National Nature Reserve office, ❸
Cafés/pubs Nearest in Bovey Tracey
Terrain Compacted gravel and earth paths

Hilliness	Undulating, with steady ascents and descents
Footwear	Winter Spring/Summer/Autumn 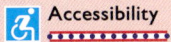
Public transport	None
Accessibility	Suitable throughout for powered wheelchairs and all-terrain pushchairs
Dogs	Welcome but keep on leads. No stiles

Did you know? Bovey Tracey parish church is dedicated to Saints Peter, Paul and Thomas of Canterbury. Sir William Tracey, one-time owner of the Parke Estate, was serving King Henry II in Normandy in 1170 when the king uttered – referring to Archbishop Thomas à Becket – 'Who will rid me of this turbulent priest?' Sir William Tracey and three other knights arrived in Canterbury on 29 December. The archbishop refused to be taken prisoner; it was Tracey who first wielded his sword.

Local legends The ancient cross in Manaton churchyard may once have been a waymark cross, located elsewhere. Legend has it that it was traditional to carry every coffin around the original churchyard cross three times before entering the church. In the mid-1880s a new vicar wanted his parishioners to stop this heretical practice. When they refused, he is thought to have destroyed the cross, or hidden it. Seventy years later the current cross was found (in use as a lintel) and installed in the churchyard.

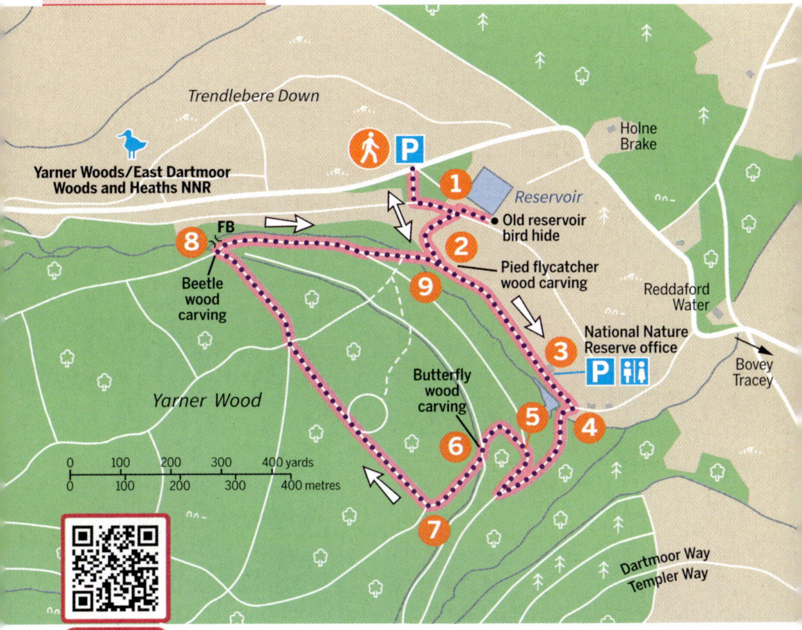

Walk 3 Yarner Wood

STORIES BEHIND THE WALK

The Parke Estate The National Trust's Parke Estate, home to Dartmoor National Park Authority, is on the outskirts of Bovey Tracey. Parke House is Grade II-listed and was rebuilt in 1826–8 by William Hole. The estate is home to the Dartmoor Pony Heritage Trust, which works to secure the future of the Dartmoor pony. Visitors can wander around the grounds, enjoy refreshments at the café and take a look at the produce growing in the walled garden and orchard.

Bovey Potteries A leat (man-made water course) runs through Yarner Wood and once supplied water to the Pottery Pond in Bovey Tracey, which stored water to power five waterwheels at the world-famous Bovey Potteries (1775–1956). The potteries focused on producing earthenware, using local clay (decomposed granite) laid down in the Bovey Basin. Three kilns remain at the House of Marbles on Pottery Road, where there is also a pottery museum.

P Middle Trendlebere car park

❶ Old reservoir bird hide (100 yards, left)

❷ Pied flycatcher wood carving

Yarner Wood/East Dartmoor Woods and Heaths NNR

- **Cross** the road from the car park and take the path opposite to the gate into Yarner Wood.
- Through the gate the path leads to a T-junction.
- Turn **left** on the track for 75 yards to a broad junction and information board.

❶
- For the old reservoir bird hide (100 yards), keep ahead a few paces then turn up **left**.
- Otherwise, bear **right**, downhill, and go through a gate. Descend to a track T-Junction by a wooden carving (pied flycatcher).

30   Short Walks Made Easy

☆ Wray Valley Trail

This popular 6.75-mile multi-use trail follows the trackbed of the old Newton Abbot–Moretonhampstead railway line from Parke to Moretonhampstead, via the picturesque village of Lustleigh. The railway opened in 1866 and climbed 525 feet on its journey; charabancs would meet travellers at Moretonhampstead and transport them on to popular sites on the moor. The last passenger train ran in 1959.

🐦 East Dartmoor Woods and Heaths National Nature Reserve (NNR)

Yarner Wood was purchased by the Nature Conservancy in 1952 and became England's first national nature reserve. Over the years the protected landscape has expanded and now comprises Yarner Wood, Trendlebere Down and the River Bovey valley woodlands (Hisley, Houndtor and Pullabrook). The NNR incorporates ancient woodland and wildflower-rich wet meadows, supporting an abundance of wildlife and plants. All are open to the public, with a focus on access for all at Yarner Wood.

National Nature Reserve office ½ mile

3 ●

4 ● Bird hide and pond (right)

Sharp turn right

5 ●

4 ● Turn **right** up a concrete track, ascending steadily past lofty beeches to a sharp turning on the right in 250 yards, passing another bird hide on the way (left).

● Take the sharp **right** turn, meeting a fork in 150 yards.

6 Butterfly wood carving

2 ● Branch **left** to reach the National Nature Reserve office in 300 yards.

3 ● Keep **straight ahead** through a gate, walk across a parking area and pass a bird hide overlooking a pond to meet a track junction (cottages in view ahead).

NATURE NOTES

A mature oak tree supports around 2,300 different species: birds, bryophytes, fungi, invertebrates, lichens and mammals. Yarner Wood's ancient sessile oak woodland is home to bats and dormice, and is renowned for its breeding population of pied flycatchers. It has a huge variety of woodland birds: willow warbler, chiffchaff, common redstart, lesser spotted woodpecker and blackcap, to name but a few.

In early spring look out for delicate snowdrops. In summer make sure to visit the old reservoir, where 'islands' of purple loosestrife and meadowsweet brighten the scene. And in autumn, see if you can find a very special fungus growing on a decaying bit of damp wood among the leaf litter: scarlet elf cup, a food source for rodents and slugs.

Dartmoor is home to Britain's biggest species of slug, the black ash, which can grow up to a foot long!

Oak leaves

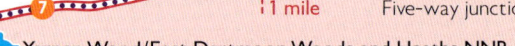

Yarner Wood/East Dartmoor Woods and Heaths NNR

5 ▪ Fork **left**, soon following the track round a sharp left bend and continuing to a crossways marked by a butterfly carving.

6 ▪ Keep **straight on** at the staggered path crossroads to rise steadily for 150 yards to a track junction.

7 ▪ Bear **right** and stay with the track to a five-way junction in ¼ mile.
▪ Go **straight on** at the junction, descending into a valley to reach a wooden shelter and a beetle carving at a track junction.

Top left: scarlet elf cup
Above: black ash slug
Left: pied flycatcher
Below: purple loosestrife

🐦 Yarner Wood/East Dartmoor Woods and Heaths NNR

8 …eetle wood carving

1½ miles

9 Pied flycatcher wood carving

Middle Trendlebere car park

8 ➡ Turn **right**, gently downhill, passing a footbridge and continuing to a fork in 300 yards.
➡ Keep **left** at the fork and go on to cross a stream and return to the pied flycatcher carving.

9 ➡ Turn sharp **left**, uphill, passing through a gate and bearing left at the next track junction (for the old reservoir bird hide) to retrace your steps to the car park.

Walk 3 Yarner Wood 33

WALK 4

HAYTOR QUARRY AND TRAMWAY

Beginning at Dartmoor National Park Visitor Centre, this is a gentle stroll across open moorland. The route leads to the abandoned Haytor Quarry, the largest of several early 19th-century granite quarries in the area, and then follows the granite tramway, with far-reaching views across a tor-studded landscape. The tramway dates from 1820 and was built to carry rock to the Stover Canal, for onward transport to Teignmouth on the south coast. Look out for ponies and cattle; listen for skylarks and ravens.

OS information
SX 765771 Explorer OL28
Distance 1.8 miles / 2.9 km
Time 1¼ hours
Start/Finish Haytor
Parking TQ13 9XT Dartmoor National Park Visitor Centre car park
Public toilets At the visitor centre
Cafés/pubs Moorland Hotel and The Rock Inn, Haytor Vale
Terrain Grassy paths; stony tracks
Hilliness One gentle ascent ❶ to ❷ and corresponding descent
Footwear Winter 🥾 Spring/Summer/Autumn 👟

Did you know? The coming of the railway to Bovey Tracey (and on to Moretonhampstead) in 1866 heralded the start of Haytor Rock's appeal as a tourist attraction, with passengers transported to the moor from the station by charabanc. Mercifully, an early 20th-century scheme to construct a coal-fired electric tramway to improve access to the rocks came to naught.

Local legend It is said that Hound Tor (in view ④ to ⑤) comprises a pack of hounds, turned into stone in the 11th century when the hunter Bowerman disturbed a coven of witches. In revenge, they encased him and his hounds in stone. To this day Bowerman – a 40-foot stack of granite, known locally as 'Bowerman's Nose' – stands on nearby Hayne Down.

Public transport
Limited bus services 193, between Bovey Tracey and Newton Abbot, and 271, between Newton Abbot and Widecombe, stopping in Haytor Vale: countrybusdevon.co.uk; Haytor Hoppa (summer Saturdays from Newton Abbot railway station): stagecoachbus.com

Accessibility
Powered wheelchair and pushchair friendly ① to ③ and then via accessible shortcut from ⑥ to end

Dogs
Welcome, but keep on leads 1 March to 31 July and under close control at all times. No stiles

Walk 4 Haytor Quarry and Tramway 35

STORIES BEHIND THE WALK

☆ **The quarrymen and their families** Around 100 men worked at Haytor Quarry during its heyday; there were several more quarries on Haytor Down, including a large one below Holwell Tor. George Templer built cottages, a pub and, possibly, a school for his workers; traces of walls and embankments can be seen near the route at ❺. In 1825 more cottages were built in Haytor Vale; the Rock Inn was originally the hostel for single working men.

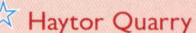

☆ **Haytor Quarry**
Commercial quarrying began on Haytor Down around 1820 under the ownership of George Templer (1781–1843), who lived at Stover, to the south of the moor. Haytor Quarry was expanded in 1825 when it won the contract for supplying granite for work at the British Museum and for the arches of London Bridge. It fell largely into disuse around 1865 due to granite being sourced more cheaply from Cornwall.

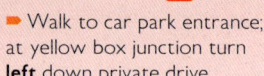 View to Haytor Rocks (left)

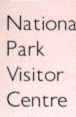

National Park Visitor Centre car park

▶ Walk to car park entrance; at yellow box junction turn **left** down private drive.
▶ Halfway along, turn **right** through a line of small boulders onto a grassy swathe, parallel to road. 100 yards before car park ahead, turn **right** to road with stony track opposite.

❶ ▶ **Cross** the road to follow the broad, rising track (Miles Without Stiles route). The eastern outcrop of Haytor Rocks is ahead left.
▶ Climb towards spoil heaps edging Haytor Quarry to reach a gate, just after crossing the Dartmoor Way long-distance path.

Short Walks Made Easy

☆ **Granite Tramway** The first of its kind in Devon, the granite tramway ran for 8 miles from Haytor Down to the head of the Stover Canal at Teigngrace. Granite was transported in horse-drawn trucks. The canal was built by George Templer's father James, opening in 1790 to transport ball clay from his workings around the Bovey Basin. Today the route of the tramway forms the basis of the 18-mile Templer Way walk, which finishes at Shaldon, at the mouth of the River Teign.

🐦 **Emsworthy Mire**
A Devon Wildlife Trust reserve, Emsworthy Mire is locally famous for its magnificent display of bluebells in May. At its heart lie the ruins of a moorland farm, abandoned since the 1870s. Keep your eyes peeled and you may be lucky enough to find a sundew growing in the damp ground beneath your feet, or spot a damselfly dancing over one of the ponds. A waymarked route runs round the reserve (please keep dogs on leads).

Haytor Quarry ½ mile

Accessible route turns right

Granite Tramway

2 ▸ Pass through the gate, heading **left** along a good path; the gulley, below right, was an extension to the main quarry.
▸ Arrive at the quarry ponds then follow the path round the water's edge to a gate in the north boundary.

3 ▸ Exit via the gate, passing between heather- and whortleberry- covered spoil heaps, to reach a path junction: the accessible route bears **right** here to rejoin the main route beyond **5**.
▸ Otherwise, keep **ahead** on a broad path to reach the granite tramway.

Walk 4 Haytor Quarry and Tramway

NATURE NOTES

Haytor Down has wonderful displays of mauve ling, purple bell heather and bright yellow gorse in late summer.

Plentiful livestock graze the common here: you might spot some 'Belties' – belted Galloway cattle – characterised by their broad white girth. Another breed often seen (more typically on the higher parts of the moor) is the all-black Galloway: originating in the 17th century in South West Scotland, it is small, tough and renowned for its hardiness.

On the south moor you're more likely to find home-grown South Devon cattle, nicknamed 'orange elephants' on account of their size and colouring. On the northern edge of Dartmoor you may see deep rich reddish-brown Red Ruby cattle, which originate in the heart of the county. And – much admired (and photographed) by visitors – there are a few herds of shaggy and placid Highland cattle scattered across the commons too!

South Devon cow

Accessible route rejoins from the right

1 mile

Granite Tramway

4 ▬ Turn **right** along the flanged granite rails. Continue with the tramway as it curves right to reach a Templer Way marker stone and junction in 200 yards.

5 ▬ Turn **right**; follow the old branch line tramway towards the quarry, crossing an embankment and curving left past a junction – accessible route rejoins by a big spoil heap.

▬ Beyond a broad level area, bear right, gently uphill – Haytor comes into view ahead – to reach the approach track a few yards from the quarry gate.

38   Short Walks Made Easy

Above: Highland cow
Below: belted Galloway

Top: gorse **Bottom:** bell heather

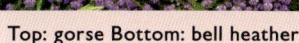

Haytor Quarry (right)

1½ miles

View to Haytor Rocks (right)

National Park Visitor Centre car park

6 ▶ Turn **left** and follow the track back to the road; **cross** over and retrace your steps to the car park.

One of Britain's largest and most spectacular insects, the emperor moth is widely spread but not commonly seen across heather moorland. A day-flying moth, it has wonderful peacock-like eyespots on all four wings.

Walk 4 Haytor Quarry and Tramway

Opposite (clockwise): lapwing; Dartmoor pony; rowan berries; common hawker
This page (clockwise): kestrel; meadowsweet; redstart

WALK 5

BELLEVER FOREST

This is an easy-going walk through a coniferous plantation and across open heathland in the heart of the national park. It utilises one of Dartmoor's 'Miles Without Stiles' initiatives, and flirts with the History Hunter Trail, which highlights sites of archaeological interest. The walk encircles Lakehead Hill, in the middle of the forest, enjoying far-reaching views north towards the old gunpowder factory at Powdermills and the ridge beyond, crowned by a line of craggy granite tors, and south to Bellever Tor.

OS information	
SX 646786 Explorer OL28	
Distance	2.4 miles/3.8 km
Time	1½ hours
Start/Finish	Bellever Forest, Postbridge
Parking	PL20 6TU Forestry England car park, on south side of B3212; turning opposite National Park Visitor Centre, Postbridge, PL20 6TH
Public toilets	At the National Park Visitor Centre
Cafés/pubs	East Dart Inn and Postbridge Stores, Postbridge
Terrain	Gravel forest tracks; rough grass and unsurfaced path ④ to ⑥
Hilliness	Gently undulating
Footwear	Year round
Public transport	Bus services 98, between Tavistock and Yelverton, and DART, between Exeter and Plymouth, stops at Postbridge: plymouthbus.co.uk; firstbus.co.uk/cornwall

Did you know? In the 1990s a prehistoric cist (grave) was discovered in a bank of peat on Whitehorse Hill, high up on the moor above Postbridge. An excavation in 2011 revealed this to be a find of international importance, dating from the Early Bronze Age and containing the cremated remains of (probably) a young female, along with a range of significant grave goods, wrapped up in a brown bear pelt and fastened with a copper alloy pin.

Local legend Anyone travelling along the road west of Postbridge needs to beware the 'Hairy Hands', which grab the steering wheel and force unwary drivers off the road! Various origins to the legend have been proposed. One talks of an Italian worker who, on returning to Powdermills gunpowder factory to pick up his tools one night, forgot to take off his steel-capped boots: a random spark caused a huge explosion. And all that was left was a pair of hairy hands...

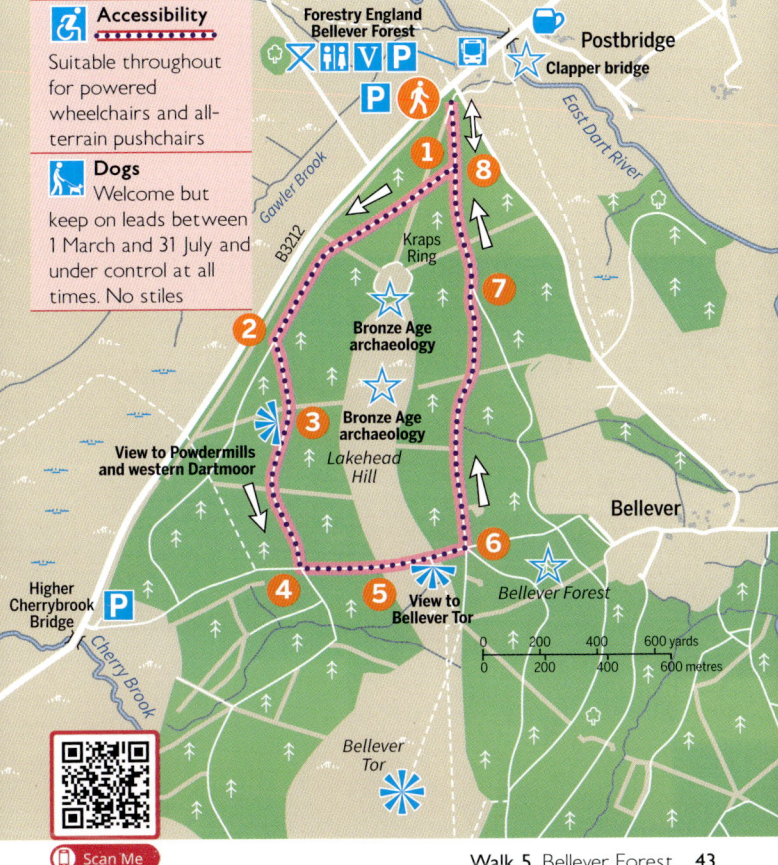

Accessibility
Suitable throughout for powered wheelchairs and all-terrain pushchairs

Dogs
Welcome but keep on leads between 1 March and 31 July and under control at all times. No stiles

Walk 5 Bellever Forest

STORIES BEHIND THE WALK

☆ **Bronze Age archaeology** Dartmoor has the greatest concentration of Bronze Age sites in the whole of North West Europe. There are more than 30 hut circles in Bellever Forest, dating from between 4,000 and 2,600 years ago; Kraps Ring, north of the summit of Lakehead Hill, is bounded by a bank of stones, and contains around 15 hut circles. There are also stone cists, burial cairns and stone rows: five sites are scheduled as being of national importance.

☆ **Bellever Forest** Owned by the Duchy of Cornwall – the largest landowner on Dartmoor – since 1337, the coniferous plantation was acquired by the Forestry Commission (now Forest England) in 1930. Increased demand for timber led to extensive planting of North American Sitka spruce, completed by 1943. Today's forest management encompasses rather broader values: planting, harvesting and re-stocking give priority to the protection of the forest's wildlife and archaeology, and far greater emphasis is given to encouraging public access.

☆ Bellever Forest

Path (left) to Kraps Ring

Bronze Age archaeology ☆

½ mile

Forestry England Bellever Forest car park (Postbridge)
- Begin by passing through the gate by the car park and head **uphill** on the broad track into a coniferous plantation to the first turning on the right in 250 yards.

① ▶ Turn right, on the History Hunter Trail (HHT) and the Cycle and Tramper Trail (CTT).
- Stay with this wide track for ½ mile to a broad track junction, passing a narrow path heading off left (HHT) on the way.

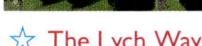

☆ Clapper Bridge

The clapper bridge at Postbridge, which crosses the East Dart River just below the road bridge, is one of the finest examples of its type in Britain. Clapper bridges date from medieval times and consist of large flat slabs of stone – 'clappers' – resting on top of stone piers. Most probably, they replaced stepping stones, and were built to help packhorses cross the river. Clapper bridges are found elsewhere in the country, but the greatest concentration is on Dartmoor.

View to Powdermills and western Dartmoor

☆ The Lych Way

Hundreds of years ago there was no consecrated ground in Postbridge; the nearest burial site was at Lydford, the most important settlement in the ancient Royal Forest and an administrative centre for Stannary Law (governing Dartmoor's tin industry) and Forest Law. Corpses were carried across the moor to Lydford, a distance of about 12 miles, on a route that became known as the 'Way of the Dead'. The Lych Way crosses Lakehead Hill then heads north onto the moor.

Lake Hill ③

1 mile

☆ B e l l e v e r   F o r e s t

② ▶ Bear **left** at the broad track junction (CTT goes straight on), gently uphill, across the western slope of Lakehead Hill, pausing at the top of the rise.

③ ▶ At the crest of the hill, take in the wonderful views westwards across the moor and descend gently through an open area (felled in 2022) to a track crossroads in ⅓ mile.

④ ▶ Turn **left** on a narrower and rougher path, re-joining the CTT, emerging from the trees in about 300 yards.

NATURE NOTES

A herd of Dartmoor heritage ponies is most likely to be seen on Lakehead Hill. Their grazing prevents important archaeological sites from becoming overgrown, and opens up the land for more species. Ponies eat young gorse shoots, trample tough gorse stems and bracken, and keep invasive purple moor grass at bay. Heritage ponies are different from the coloured ponies often seen on the moor, being closer in colouring and conformation to the registered Dartmoor pony; the breed standard for the latter was laid down in 1925.

Bellever also has a good population of nightjar, which nest in open spaces and like clear-felled sites. The goldcrest and the firecrest, Britain's most diminutive birds, inhabit the coniferous woodland. Both have very high-pitched and rhythmic, repetitive calls, and look alike but the firecrest has a distinguishing white stripe above its eyes.

On warm, dry days keep an eye out for adders basking on the path. You may also be lucky enough to spot a common lizard skittering away into cover.

Right: adder
Far right: common lizard

5 ▶ The path crosses rough grassland on the southern slope of Lakehead Hill; Bellever Tor comes into view (right).
▶ Pass through a belt of trees to reach a signed five-way track junction.

6 ▶ At the junction turn **left**, and shortly pass a path off left to a cairn circle and cist (HHT).
▶ Keep forward for ⅓ mile as the main track starts to descend gently to meet a track coming in from the right.

Dartmoor pony

Goldcrest

Above: firecrest
Below: nightjar

☆ Bellever Forest

Path (left) to Kraps Ring

2 miles

☆ Bronze Age archaeology

Forestry England Bellever Forest car park (Postbridge) 🅿

7 ▪ Keep **straight on** at the junction and continue between stands of lofty conifers, passing another burial site accessed via a narrow path (HHT), to return to the junction used earlier in the walk.

8 ▪ This time, continue **downhill**, go through the gate at the bottom and return to the car park.

WALK 6

PRINCETOWN AND FOGGINTOR QUARRY

This is a great there-and-back walk for a bright sunny day – particularly when the prevailing south-westerly winds are light. Princetown is the highest settlement on the moor, and famously home to Dartmoor Prison. As you head west along the trackbed of the old railway you'll enjoy phenomenal views; there's lots of industrial archaeology to explore as well as impressive tors to identify. The trackbed is nice and level, but bumpy in places (watch out for mountain bikes).

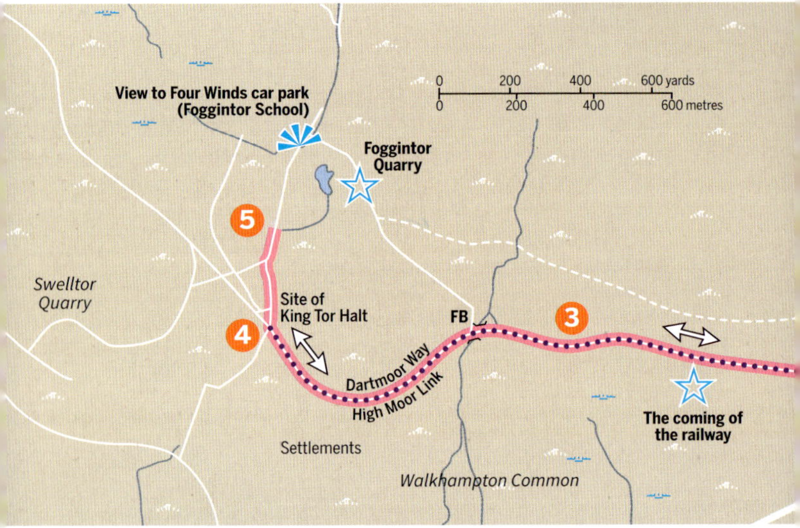

48   Short Walks Made Easy

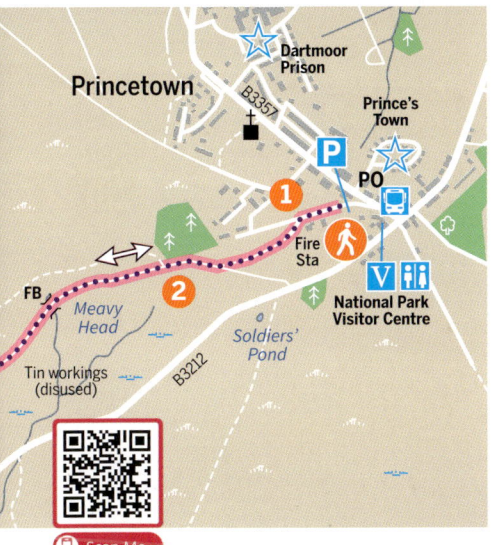

OS information

SX 589734
Explorer OL28

Distance
3.7 miles/6km

Time
2 hours

Start/Finish
Princetown

Parking PL20 6QG
Station Road car park

Public toilets
Next to Station Road car park

Cafés/pubs
Princetown

Terrain
Stony-surfaced, old railway trackbed

Hilliness
Level throughout

Footwear
Autumn/Winter
Spring/Summer

Public transport
Bus services 98, between Tavistock and Yelverton, and DART, between Exeter and Plymouth: plymouthbus.co.uk; firstbus.co.uk/cornwall

Accessibility
Powered wheelchairs and all-terrain pushchairs to ❹; the track to the quarry, ❹ to ❺, is rougher

Dogs Welcome but keep on leads between 1 March and 31 July. No stiles

Walk 6 Princetown and Foggintor Quarry 49

STORIES BEHIND THE WALK

☆ **Prince's Town** This remote settlement owes its existence largely to Sir Thomas Tyrwhitt, a close friend of the Prince Regent (later George IV). Tyrwhitt was appointed auditor to the Duchy of Cornwall in 1796 and set about developing the hamlet. He initiated the building of the prison (1806–09); he commissioned the first iron railroad built in Devon (Plymouth & Dartmoor Railway). He was also responsible for the construction of an impressive residence on his Tor Royal Estate, to the south of Princetown.

☆ **Dartmoor Prison** The prison opened in 1809 to accommodate more than 5,000 French prisoners-of-war housed in prison hulks at Devonport, Plymouth. They were later joined by PoWs from Britain's 1812 war with America. Princetown's old church was built by the Americans; some are buried in the graveyard. During World War I the prison held more than 1,000 conscientious objectors who worked on pointless local initiatives such as: the 'Conchies Road' – 'the road to nowhere' – that crosses the moor south-east of the town.

Prince's Town

Fire station

Station Road car park

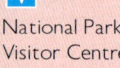
National Park Visitor Centre Princetown

Bridge over River Meavy

½ mile

The coming of the railway

■ From the car park entrance turn **left**, walking 125 yards to a path junction immediately beyond the fire station and a Station Cottages sign.

① ■ Turn **left** at the Princetown Railway Walking and Mountain Bike Route sign (old railway stable, left).
■ Keep **straight on** where another path joins from the left.
■ The way broadens and reaches the end corner of a conifer plantation (right).

☆ The coming of the railway

The Plymouth & Dartmoor Railroad opened in 1823, linking Foggintor Quarry with Crabtree Wharf; it was later extended into the middle of Princetown. The railroad transported granite from the many local quarries, including stone for Nelson's Column in Trafalgar Square. It was taken over by the Great Western Railway (as the Yelverton-to-Princetown branch line) in 1883 but was never profitable, and finally closed in 1956.

☆ Foggintor School

Look to the north from the quarry, and across the common you'll spot the trees (and low walls) marking Four Winds car park, once the site of Foggintor School, which served the children of local quarry workers. A conifer standing in the middle of the site was given to the schoolchildren one Christmas by prisoners at HMP Dartmoor. The school opened in 1915 and closed in 1936; the building was demolished in 1964.

Plymouth & Dartmoor Railroad

Cutting — 1 mile — ③ — Bridge over tributary of River Walkham — 1½ miles — Site of King Tor Halt — ④

② ▬ Continue along the old railway trackbed for ¾ mile to a cutting, on the way crossing a bridge over damp ground (the source of the River Meavy).

③ ▬ Pass through the cutting and cross another bridge (over a tributary of the River Walkham).
▬ Continue for almost ½ mile as the trackbed makes a broad sweep to the right to reach a crossroads of tracks.

Walk 6 Princetown and Foggintor Quarry

NATURE NOTES

This wonderfully airy route introduces walkers to Dartmoor's more common moorland birds: skylark, wheatear, stonechat, Dartford warbler and perhaps buzzard and raven.

With a wingspan of up to 4 feet, the buzzard is a medium-sized raptor typically seen soaring high in the sky and, on sunny days, wheeling round on currents of warm air that rise up off the moor.

Efforts are being made to restore areas of open water and blanket bog on the higher moor in the hope of increasing populations of curlew, snipe, dunlin and lapwing, all rarely seen on Dartmoor today.

The lapwing is also known as the peewit, after its very distinctive call.

The most common sheep breed seen right across the moor is the Scottish blackface. There is ongoing and enthusiastic support for increasing stock levels of traditional local breeds such as the whiteface Dartmoor, greyface Dartmoor, and Devon and Cornwall longwool, with encouraging results.

Above: lapwing
Opposite top: greyface Dartmoor
Opposite bottom: snipe

Plymouth & Dartmoor Railroad

Foggintor Quarry

Site of King Tor Halt

2 miles

Bridge over tributary of River Walkham

Cutting

2½ miles

Did you know? Foggintor Quarry started life as Royal Oak Quarry, and was worked from 1820 for around 80 years. Huge spoil heaps and the remains of numerous structures dot the area, including the dramatic remnants of Hill Cottages, demolished in 1953. At one time, 30 cottages housed quarry workers hereabouts. By an old siding at Swelltor Quarry lie some granite corbels, cut in 1903 for use in the construction of London Bridge, but surplus to requirements.

Local legend Dartmoor's supposedly bottomless bogs play a big part in all manner of eerie tales and moorland legends. A couple of miles to the south of Princetown, down the Eylesbarrow track, stands an empty and desolate farmhouse near Siward's (Nun's) Cross. Nun's Cross Farm is on the edge of the infamous Foxtor Mires, immortalised as Grimpen Mire in Sherlock Holmes' tale of *The Hound of the Baskervilles*.

Above: whiteface Dartmoor
Below: wheatear (juvenile)

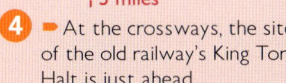

The coming of the railway — Bridge over River Meavy — 3 miles — 3½ miles — Fire station — Prince's Town — Station Road car park 🅿️🅿️ — National Park Visitor Centre

4 ▶ At the crossways, the site of the old railway's King Tor Halt is just ahead.
▶ Turn **right** on a rough track to arrive at the first entrance (right) to abandoned Foggintor Quarry in about 200 yards, keeping **forward** to the second entrance in another 75 yards.

5 ▶ The path from the second entrance leads to the quarry pond.
▶ Having enjoyed the views around the quarry, about-turn and retrace your steps along the railway trackbed back to Princetown.

Walk 6 Princetown and Foggintor Quarry

WALK 7

RAF HARROWBEER

Go for a walk across Roborough Down, west of Yelverton, and you'll encounter grassed-over embankments, bunkers and concrete standings. In World War II this area was home to a military airfield; at one time 2,000 personnel served here. There were three runways, parts of which can still be traced on the close-cropped sward (you'll come across a lot of livestock on this walk). This level and easy route explores the airfield and enjoys wonderful views over Dartmoor's western tors.

OS information
SX 518679 Explorer OL28
Distance 2.4 miles/3.8km
Time 1½ hours
Start/Finish Yelverton
Parking PL20 6DJ Leg o' Mutton Corner car park
Public toilets Yelverton long-stay car park
Cafés/pubs Dartmoor Bakery at Yelverton
Terrain Grassy paths across common
Hilliness Level throughout (former airfield)
Footwear Winter 🥾 Spring/Summer/Autumn 👟
Public transport Bus services 1, between Plymouth and Tavistock; 98, between Tavistock and Yelverton; and DART, between Exeter and Plymouth: stagecoachbus.com; plymouthbus.co.uk; firstbus.co.uk/cornwall

54   Short Walks Made Easy

Did you know? There's an interesting story behind Yelverton's row of single-storey shops – the top floor was removed as they were on the direct flight path from RAF Harrowbeer, which opened on Roborough Down in 1941 after the Plymouth blitz, officially closing in July 1945. There's a fascinating archive at the former control tower, **8**, and the RAF Harrowbeer Interest Group holds a nostalgic 1940s weekend on the site every August.

Local legend The picturesque village of Meavy, 1½ miles east of Yelverton, has a replica of Drake's Drum, housed in the gable of the primary school. Sir Francis Drake lived at nearby Buckland Abbey, where the original drum is kept (saved from his fatal last voyage in 1596). Rumour has it that the drum will sound if England's safety is threatened.

Accessibility

For powered wheelchairs there's an awkward bank at **2** but in dry conditions the rest of the route is accessible, with alternative parking at **5** and **8** to **9**. Suitable for all-terrain pushchairs throughout

Dogs
Welcome but keep on leads. No stiles

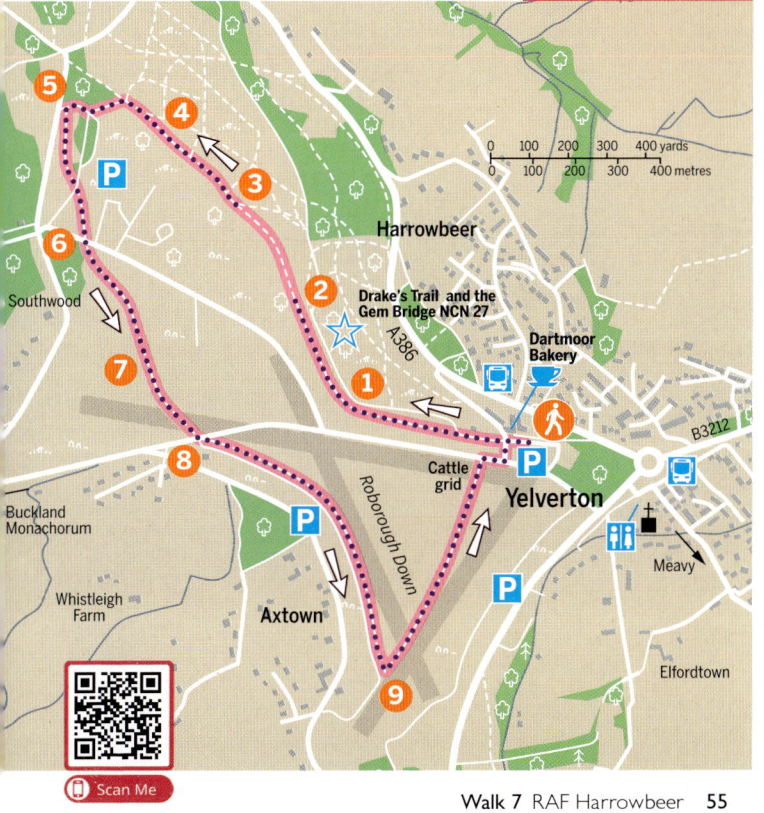

Walk 7 RAF Harrowbeer

STORIES BEHIND THE WALK

☆ Drake's Trail and the Gem Bridge
National Cycle Route 27 links Devon's south and north coasts, and here follows the Drake's Trail along the edge of Roborough Down. A few miles north the route – following the former Plympton to Tavistock railway line – crosses the River Walkham on the impressive Gem Bridge, opened in 2012 and towering 80 feet over the wooded valley. The original Isambard Kingdom Brunel viaduct was built for the railway in 1859 and demolished in 1965, following its closure.

☆ Tamar Valley Area of Outstanding Natural Beauty
This stunningly beautiful area, on the Devon/Cornwall border, comprises the River Tamar and its valley, and sections of the rivers Tavy and Lynher. It includes a wide estuary landscape edged with wetlands; a tidal middle valley with creeks and wooded valley slopes; a mining heritage dating back to medieval times; a market garden and orchard legacy; and landscaped estates. It has quays, limekilns, old ferry points and historic stone bridges, and links with early medieval saints.

☆ Drake's Trail and the Gem Bridge

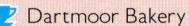

NCN 27 — Old runway end — ½ mile

🅿 Leg o' Mutton Corner car park
☕ Dartmoor Bakery

▶ From the car park entrance, **cross** the road to the tarmac path ahead (Drake's Trail: NCN 27).
▶ Pass through two gates onto the common.
▶ Drake's Trail soon bears right; here keep **straight on** alongside trees to reach an old runway end in 300 yards.

❶ ▶ Bear **right**, still alongside trees, for another 300 yards to a low bank at the far end of the old runway.
▶ Round the low bank then keep ahead to drop down a steeper bank by a solitary ash tree.

Buckland Abbey

A Cistercian monastery founded in the late 13th century — the last one built in medieval England and Wales — the abbey fell foul of Henry VIII's Reformation (the Great Barn is a survivor from that time). Later in the 16th century it was developed into an impressive mansion, home to Sir Richard Grenville and then Sir Francis Drake, the first Englishman to circumnavigate the globe (1577–80). Buckland Abbey is now in the hands of the National Trust (nationaltrust.org.uk).

The Garden House

Located on the edge of the Tamar Valley to the west of Yelverton, this is a beautiful spot (open to the public; thegardenhouse.org.uk). The site's history dates back to 1305 when it became the vicarage to the neighbouring village of Buckland Monachorum. In the summer of 1945, Lionel and Katharine Fortescue moved here from their home at Eton College, renaming it The Garden House. Lionel spent his retirement developing a beautiful 10-acre garden, complete with decorative borders, an arboretum and formal lawns.

Six-way junction

2 ■ Follow the grassy way **ahead**, between bracken and stands of gorse.
■ Keep **straight on** at the next junction of paths, passing close to a tree-filled gulley (right) and enjoying wonderful views of Dartmoor to reach a broad and obvious fork.

3 ■ Keep **right** at the fork, on the narrower path, to pass a solitary oak tree.
■ Keep **straight on** at the next path crossroads to reach a broad, six-way junction.

4 ■ At the junction (the path right drops away steeply), take the **left** of two paths ahead, passing through closely spaced oak and hawthorn trees.
■ At a path junction in 150 yards, turn **left** towards a parking area.

Walk 7 RAF Harrowbeer

NATURE NOTES

Roborough Down is home to large numbers of sheep and Dartmoor hill ponies. The latter come in all sizes and colours: the higher you go on the moor, the smaller and hardier the ponies tend to be. Coloured ponies (black and white or brown and white), often seen at Harrowbeer, have been on the moor since medieval times, according to historic records.

In May the plentiful hawthorn trees along the route will be dressed in wonderful frothy white blossom. Tough, twisted hawthorns dot the lower slopes all across the moor: the red berries have traditionally been used to treat heart disease and digestive problems.

The red-orange berries of rowan (mountain ash) trees add to the colour palette in the autumn months.

In summertime the close-cropped grassland is dotted with brilliant yellow hawkbit, with occasional patches of low-growing and fragrant wild thyme.

Kestrels may be seen over the open common, hovering in one position studying the ground intently for any tell-tale movements of small mammals, their favourite prey.

Aim for the cream-coloured house ahead ⑦ Road ⑧ Former aircraft dispersal bays (right

1½ miles

⑤ ▶ Just before reaching the road, turn **left** on a grassy path.
▶ Keep **left** at an early fork.
▶ **Cross** a stony track; keep **straight on** to reach the road by another parking area.

⑥ ▶ **Cross** the road and turn **left** and keep **straight on**, passing to the left of concrete standings.
▶ Continue in the same direction through stands of gorse, eventually passing two more areas of hardstanding to emerge onto the open common.

⑦ ▶ **Cross** the common, heading towards a cream-coloured house partly concealed by trees.
▶ Reach the road and cross over.

Above: hawkbit
Below: kestrel

Top: Dartmoor hill ponies
Bottom: hawthorn

Old control tower/
RAF Harrowbeer
Archives (right)

Aim for North Hessary Tor transmitter mast (ahead)

Dartmoor Bakery

Cattle grid

2 miles

Roborough Down

Leg o'Mutton Corner car park

8 ▸ Turn **left**, keeping to the grassy sward parallel to a tarmac way for ½ mile, passing a line of aircraft dispersal chambers, to the point where the tarmac way turns sharp right, with the old control tower (RAF Harrowbeer Archives), right.

9 ▸ Turn sharp **left** (along another runway), North Hessary Tor mast ahead.
▸ Strike out for ⅓ mile, aiming for the left end of a fence on the far side.
▸ Reach the road (cattle grid); cross over, turn **right** through a gate then **left** to the car park.

Walk 7 RAF Harrowbeer

Opposite (clockwise):
Fingle Bridge Inn; The
Old Police Station Café,
Princetown; Royal Oak
Inn, Meavy; Dartmoor
Bakery, Yelverton;
This page (clockwise):
Postbridge Stores;
The Bulleid Buffet,
Okehampton Station;
Cream tea at Bellever
Powdermills; ice cream
van at Burrator Dam

WALK 8

BURRATOR ARBORETUM

Burrator Arboretum and Nature Reserve, at the east end of Burrator Reservoir, can be explored on a Dartmoor National Park 'Miles Without Stiles' initiative short nature trail. A network of narrower paths weaves between the trees providing an easy-access figure-of-eight route that follows the Narrator Brook and visits a wildlife pond. See how many tree species you can identify, and the number of dragonflies and damselflies you can spot. The Burrator Discovery Centre, north of Burrator Dam, is well worth a visit.

OS information
SX 568689 Explorer OL28
Distance 0.7 miles/1.1km
Time ½ hour
Start/Finish Burrator Arboretum and Nature Reserve
Parking PL20 6PF Burrator Arboretum and Nature Reserve car park
Public toilets Nearest at the west end of Burrator Reservoir dam
Cafés/pubs Nearest: Royal Oak Inn, Meavy; ice cream van at Burrator Reservoir dam
Terrain Surfaced tracks (compacted aggregate) and boardwalk

Hilliness	Level throughout
Footwear	Year round 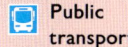
Public transport	None
Accessibility	Wheelchair and pushchair friendly
Dogs	Welcome but keep on leads between 1 March and 31 July and under control at all times. No stiles

Did you know? Traces of Burrator & Sheepstor Halt, on the old Great Western Railway line between Princetown and Yelverton, can still be identified today close to the west end of Burrator Dam: look out for isolated fence posts and the concrete-and-brick foundations of the original wooden shelter. The halt opened in 1924 and provided access for those working on the extension of the reservoir, necessary to increase capacity to over one million gallons. The halt was closed in 1956.

Local legends Crazywell Pool is a flooded mineworking 1¼ miles north-east of the arboretum, but its remote location has given rise to all manner of stories. Some believe it to be tidal, linked to the sea at Plymouth by a tunnel; others believe it to be bottomless. It is also said that on Midsummer's Eve the reflection of the next person to die in Walkhampton parish will be reflected in its dark waters, accompanied by a wailing voice calling out the unfortunate's name!

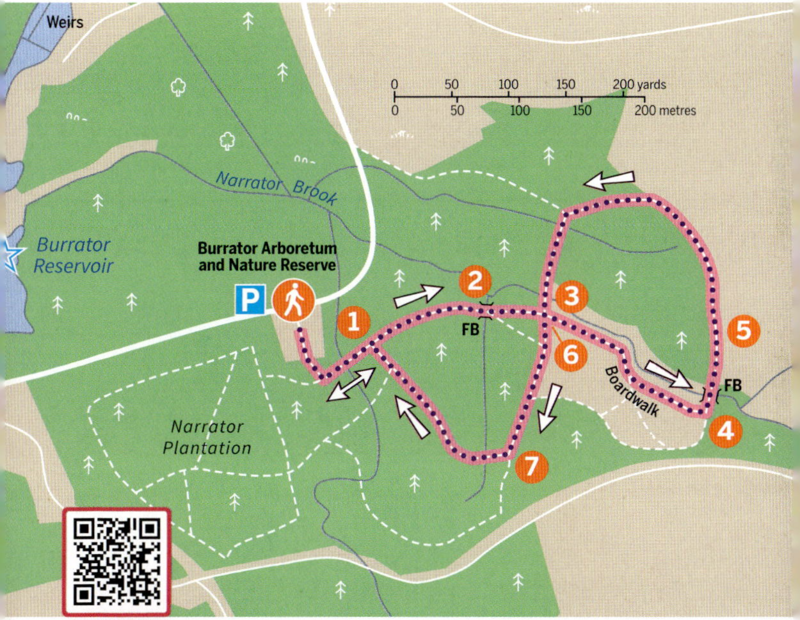

Walk 8 Burrator Arboretum

STORIES BEHIND THE WALK

⭐ **Burrator Reservoir** The reservoir was built 1893–8, and enlarged in the 1920s; a temporary suspension bridge was constructed to/from Sheepstor while the road across the dam was out of operation. Burrator's catchment area is the watershed of the Upper Meavy river, a basin that has been supplying Plymouth with water since 1591 via the 17-mile-long Drake's (Plymouth) Leat, now under the reservoir's waters.

❄ **Burrator farms and potato cave**
Plymouth Corporation purchased the majority of the land surrounding the reservoir prior to construction, and cleared it of both people and farm animals in 1916 in response to concerns about pollution; the ruined walls and buildings of 16 farms dot the landscape. William Pengelly refused to leave Combeshead Farm and stayed until his death in 1931; he was the last person to live in the catchment area. A so-called potato cave or 'hull' can still be found within the Combeshead ruins.

Burrator Arboretum and Nature Reserve

❶ ❷ Footbridge ❸

Burrator Arboretum and
Nature Reserve car park

▸ Pass through the gate at the end of the car park, entering the arboretum and following a track, which bears **left** to a path junction.

❶ ▸ Keep **straight on** to reach a T-junction in 100 yards.

64 Short Walks Made Easy

⭐ Devonport Leat

As the population of Plymouth increased, so did the demand for water. The Devonport Leat was constructed 1793–1801; it now feeds into Burrator Reservoir, but the leat channel can still be identified in many places below the dam. The leat ran from its take-off point on the West Dart river, above Two Bridges, to Devonport town and dockyard. Its waters are still carried across the rivers Cowsic and Meavy, on the moor above Burrator, via small aqueducts.

✝ The White Rajahs of Sarawak

The delightful 15th-century church of St Leonard's in Sheepstor has a surprise in store for visitors: it is the burial place of three of the White Rajahs of Sarawak (the largest of Malaysia's 13 states). Burrator House, to the south of the dam, was home to the first White Rajah, Sir James Brooke, from 1859 to 1868. He became churchwarden at St Leonard's, and styled himself as 'Lord of the Manor of Sheepstor'. He is buried in the churchyard.

Narrator Brook — Footbridge ❹ — ¼ mile — Pond and viewing platform ❺

Boardwalk

Burrator Arboretum and Nature Reserve

❷ ▸ Turn **left** towards a bridge over the Narrator Brook.
▸ **Cross** the bridge and continue 75 yards to the next junction.

❸ ▸ With the pretty stream on your left, pick up and follow a wide boardwalk for 150 yards.

Walk 8 Burrator Arboretum

NATURE NOTES

Stop for a while at one of the ponds in the arboretum, edged with spreads of pretty water forget-me-not.

See if you can spot any dragonflies and their smaller relatives, damselflies: common hawkers and emperor dragonflies, emerald and azure damselflies can all be seen here.

Water boatmen and pond skaters balance lightly on the surface of the pond, home too to common frogs, common toads and palmate newts.

The varied tree species in the arboretum support a great range of woodland birds, including nuthatch, robin and wren.

The sweet chestnut is a deciduous tree that can be long-lived and grow to over 100 feet tall. Older specimens have deeply grooved bark. In spring, they have long pale yellow catkin-like flowers. The chestnuts develop inside prickly cases and, roasted, provide a traditional Christmas treat.

On the reservoir look out for goosanders, Canada geese and mallard, as well as cormorants, perched in a row on the floating barrier above the dam.

Cormorant

Burrator Arboretum and Nature Reserve

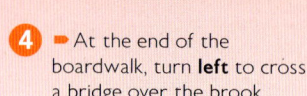
½ mile

6 Start of the boardwalk

5 ➤ At the pond, pause at the viewing platform to enjoy the insect life.
➤ Stay on the access-for-all path for 300 yards as it arcs round to the left to meet the start of the boardwalk used earlier.

4 ➤ At the end of the boardwalk, turn **left** to cross a bridge over the brook.
➤ Keep **forward** to a pond on the left in 50 yards.

66 Short Walks Made Easy

Top left: sweet chestnut
Bottom left: pond skater
Above: robin
Below: wren

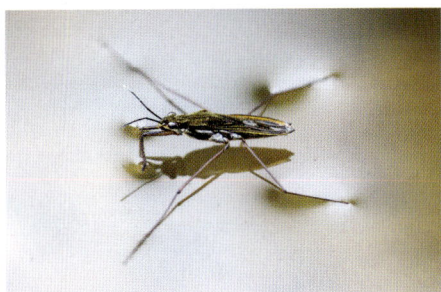

Burrator Arboretum and Nature Reserve

7

Burrator Arboretum and Nature Reserve car park 🅿

6 ▶ Keep **straight on** for 125 yards to a point where the trail bears right, passing turnings on the right and then on the left on the way.

7 ▶ Bear **right** with the path and descend very gently through a plantation of conifers for 175 yards to reach the outward route at a T-junction.
▶ Turn **left** back to the car park.

Walk 8 Burrator Arboretum

WALK 9

SHIPLEY BRIDGE AND THE AVON DAM

The Avon Dam Reservoir was completed in 1957 to supply water to Devon's South Hams. Its waters are surrounded by a vast expanse of open moor, unlike other moorland reservoirs, more usually edged by dark coniferous plantations. This very easy walk – one of Dartmoor National Park's 'Miles Without Stiles' routes – offers the chance to get that 'right out there in the middle of nowhere' feeling, without taking a step off a broad tarmac way! The route is shared with the Dartmoor Way (long-distance walking route) from soon after to .

OS information	
SX 680629 Explorer OL28	
Distance	3.7 miles/5.9km
Time	2 hours
Start/Finish	Shipley Bridge
Parking TQ10 9EL	Avon Dam car park, 2½ miles north-west of South Brent
Public toilets	Avon Dam car park
Cafés/pubs	Picnic tables at 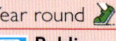, and 6
Terrain	Tarmac track
Hilliness	Gentle ascent/descent to/from the foot of the dam, with a steeper rise/fall to/from the reservoir
Footwear	Year round
Public transport	None
Accessibility	Wheelchair and pushchair friendly to 7; rough paths from 5 and 7 to the top of the dam
Dogs	Welcome but keep on leads – shared-use cycle path. No stiles

68 Short Walks Made Easy

Did you know? The Abbot's Way crosses the Avon above the reservoir. It is said to be a historic route between the abbey at Buckfast and those at Tavistock and Buckland on the west side of the moor (although there is no evidence that it was ever used by monks travelling between the two holy sites!). It is marked in places by stone crosses — Huntingdon Cross dates from the 16th century and is a boundary marker for Brent Moor.

Local legend The ruins of Holy Trinity Church — destroyed by arson in 1922 — overlook the nearby town of Buckfastleigh. In the graveyard stands the caged tomb of the infamous Squire Richard Cabell, Lord of the Manor of Brook, said to have sold his soul to the devil; his ghost roams the moors at night with his evil whisht hounds. Cabell is thought to have inspired the character of Hugo Baskerville in Arthur Conan Doyle's Sherlock Holmes story, *The Hound of the Baskervilles*.

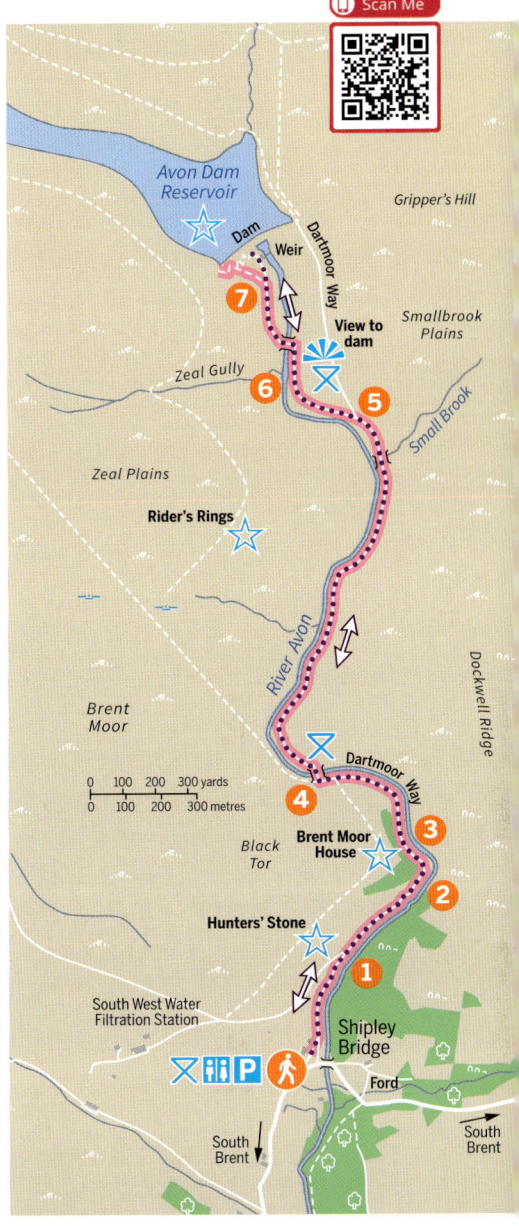

Walk 9 Shipley Bridge and the Avon Dam

STORIES BEHIND THE WALK

☆ **Hunters' Stone** Look closely and you'll see that a large boulder on the left of the track by the turning to the filtration station is engraved with a number of names and dates: these men were all distinguished members of the South Devon Hunt. It is attributed to CA Mohun Harris, who lived at Brent Moor House in the late 19th century. The boulder was moved here from its original position in 1954 during construction of the Avon Dam and reservoir.

☆ **Brent Moor House** The walk passes an area of low walls, all that remains of a large Victorian granite property that once stood on the banks of the River Avon. The house, along with 3,000 acres of moorland, was bought by Francis Meynell in 1855. The Meynell's daughter Mary died at the age of four in 1863 from acute tonsillitis and laryngitis; her memorial stands on a rocky bluff by the tarmac track. The house fell into disrepair and was demolished in the 1960s.

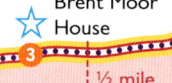
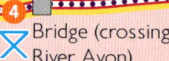

Avon Dam car park

Dartmoor Way

- Pass the toilets at the far end of the car park and carry on to meet the tarmac access lane leading to the dam, opposite the River Avon.
- Turn **left** and follow the river upstream.

1
- In about 250 yards, pass the Hunters' Stone and the lane leading to South West Water filtration station.
- Continue with the gentle ascent, river to the right, to a gate in 300 yards.

Short Walks Made Easy

⭐ **Industrial history** The car park is on the site of the former Brent Moor china clay works, which overlie an earlier naphtha works, dating from 1847. Naphtha was extracted from peat, which was cut near Red Lake high up on the south moor and transported here via the horse-drawn Zeal Tor tramway. By the mid-1850s clay was being worked on Brent Moor, and brought to the works via open channels and pipes. The works were abandoned by the 1880s.

⭐ **Rider's Rings** Dartmoor has the greatest concentration of Bronze Age sites in north-west Europe: standing stones, stone rows, hut circles, burial cists and evidence of settlements. High up on slopes of Zeal Plains on the west side of the Avon valley lie the remains of Rider's Rings, a large Bronze Age settlement thought to have contained around three dozen hut circles. Much of the enclosing wall can still be seen today.

② ▸ Go through the gate to enter the old Brent Moor Estate.
▸ Just before passing tall conifers, look left to spot the memorial to Mary Meynell.
▸ Continue to the ruins of Brent Moor House.

③ ▸ Go past the ruins, situated in a sheltered location below Black Tor, and carry on for ¼ mile to reach a bridge.

Walk 9 Shipley Bridge and the Avon Dam 71

NATURE NOTES

Dartmoor is a stronghold for the cuckoo. These opportunistic birds overwinter in the Congo rainforest; after their long journey back to Dartmoor they often usurp a meadow pipit's nest, concealed in vegetation on the ground. The cuckoo's iconic call echoes across the valley in April and May.

Look out for evidence of otters in the form of black, tarry, sweet-smelling spraint on riverside boulders.

Dense stands of rhododendron cover the riverbank near the ruins of Brent Moor House, while primroses dot the verges in spring.

Grassy paths through the bracken-covered slopes host delightful dog violets, the single food source for caterpillars of the dark green fritillary butterfly.

Clumps of compact rush, identified by the domes of flower heads on the sides of the stems, can be seen on the lower slopes as you head up the valley.

Dark green fritillary

4 ➤ Bear **right** to cross the river, passing a picnic table, and keep walking up the valley for ¾ mile to a track junction, reached soon after crossing Small Brook.

5 ➤ At the junction, you can fork **right** on the Dartmoor Way and follow it to the top of the dam (⅓ mile each way) to take a look at the reservoir.
➤ Otherwise, keep **left** on the tarmac drive to reach another picnic table.

Above: compact rush
Middle: dog violet
Bottom: cuckoo

Otter

Bridge (crossing River Avon) — 3 miles

Brent Moor House

Hunters' Stone — 3½ miles

River Avon

Avon Dam car park

6 ▸ At the picnic table, there's a good view upriver to the dam.
▸ Continue on the access lane to cross the river and reach the bottom of the dam.

7 ▸ A rough path heads off **left** up to the top of the dam for a view of the reservoir.
▸ After enjoying the scene, retrace your steps down the Avon valley to the start point.

WALK 10

LONGTIMBER WOODS

CATCH A BUS

OS information	
SX 635568 Explorer OL28	
Distance	1.7 miles/2.7km
Time	1 hour
Start/Finish	Station Road, Ivybridge
Parking PL21 0AG	Roadside on Station Road, just below the viaduct
Public toilets	None en route; nearest, Leonards Road car park, Ivybridge
Cafés/pubs	Riverside picnic table at ③; Ivybridge
Terrain	Broad woodland path 🚶 to ③; rocky and wet paths ⑤ to ⑦
Hilliness	Gradual ascent 🚶 to ⑤; steep climb from ⑤
Footwear	🚶 to ⑤ Autumn/Winter 👢; Spring/Summer 👟; ⑤ to end: year round 👢

This delightful woodland walk is alongside the beautiful River Erme, enhanced by the sound of the sparkling waters rushing away from Dartmoor's granite heart via a succession of waterfalls and deep pools. It's one of Dartmoor National Park's 'Miles Without Stiles' routes and is followed to a riverside picnic area; the optional extension continues upstream then ascends steeply through the trees, before a return via the rocky and wet Kings Gutter path. The riverside stretch is a popular dog walk.

Short Walks Made Easy

Did you know?

Across the slopes of Western Beacon, looming over the town to the north, runs the trackbed of the former Redlake Tramway. It officially opened in 1911 and was built to carry workers and equipment across the moor to china clay workings at Redlake and Leftlake Mires. Clay was transported via pipeline to the processing plant at the Cantrell Works. By the early 1930s supplies were exhausted and the track was removed.

Public transport
Bus services 20/20A from Plymouth to Ivybridge Town Hall, ½ mile south of ①: plymouthbus.co.uk

Accessibility
Suitable for powered wheelchair and all-terrain pushchairs from ① to ③

Dogs
Welcome, but under control at all times. One stile at ⑥

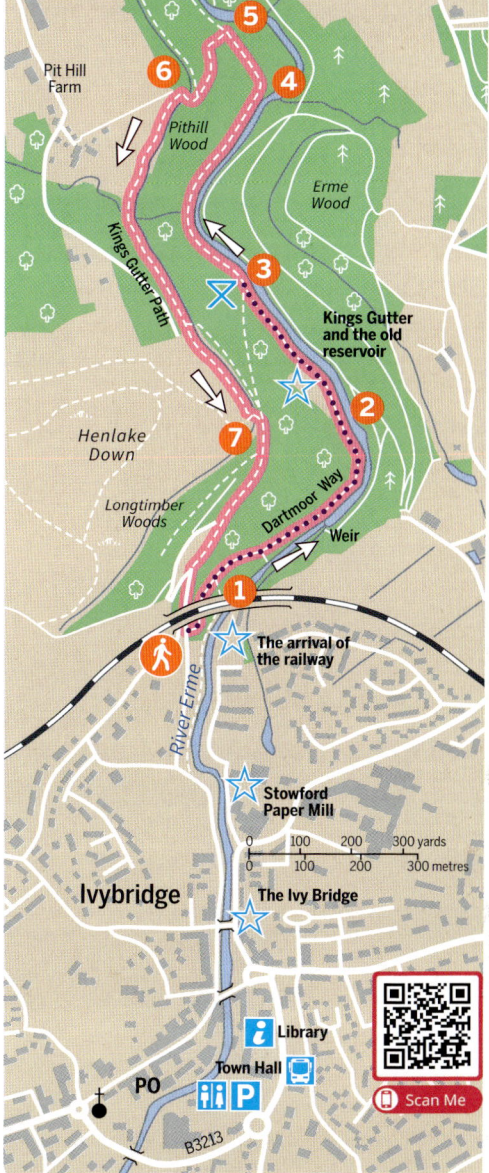

Walk 10 Longtimber Woods

STORIES BEHIND THE WALK

☆ **Stowford Paper Mill** The impressive remnants of Stowford Paper Mill sit on the east bank of the river downstream of Longtimber Woods in Ivybridge. The first paper mill was built in 1787; a corn mill had operated at the site since the 1550s. In 1849 – a year after the arrival of the railway – the mill was sold to John Allen, who carried out a lengthy renovation, completed in 1867. The business finally closed in 2013, and much of the site has been converted to residential use.

☆ **Kings Gutter and the old reservoir** Dartmoor is criss-crossed by historic leats (man-made water channels), some still supplying farms and homes. Kings Gutter dates from 1818 and was one of Ivybridge's earliest water supplies. It starts on Hanger Down, north of the town, and now functions as a footpath along the top edge of the valley woodlands. A new reservoir was built by the Erme in the 1870s, and used until 1916 (stone wall remnant at ❷); it functioned as a swimming pool until the early 1970s.

The arrival of the railway
Station Road (roadside parking)

➡ Pass round the barrier to enter Longtimber Woods and walk under the railway viaduct to reach a footpath junction in 100 yards.

Dartmoor Way

Kings Gutter and the old reservoir

River Erme

❶ ➡ Keep **straight on**, alongside the river, soon passing a weir.
➡ Continue beside the river to a substantial wall on the left.

76 Short Walks Made Easy

☆ The arrival of the railway

The original viaduct crossing the valley here dated from the coming of the single-track South Devon Railway (SDR) – engineered by Isambard Kingdom Brunel – in 1848, linking Newton Abbot with Plymouth. It was built of wood on granite pillars, and was taken over by the Great Western Railway in 1876. In 1894 a wider viaduct (to carry a double-track standard-gauge line) was built next to the original: you can still see the redundant pillars of the SDR viaduct through the trees.

☆ The Ivy Bridge

The bridge after which the town takes its name crosses the River Erme downstream from Longtimber Woods; the earliest record of a bridge here dates from the 13th century. It was later immortalised by the landscape artist JMW Turner, who visited the town twice in the early 19th century. It is also the location for the Bridge Ceremony, a re-enactment held to commemorate a dispute between the villagers of Ivybridge and neighbouring Ermington.

½ mile

P i t h i l l   W o o d

R i v e r   E r m e

2 ■ Carry on for 300 yards, reaching a picnic area and path junction.

3 ■ Keep **forward** on the path through Pithill Wood above the River Erme to a path junction in 500 yards.

Walk 10 Longtimber Woods

NATURE NOTES

The plump little brown dipper is a familiar sight on Dartmoor's rivers, perched on a rock ready to dive underwater in search of food, where it uses its wings to propel itself along.

The grey squirrel inhabits the woodland here.

In late autumn you could go on a fungus foray: a couple of the more common species to try and spot are honey fungus, usually occurring on tree stumps or on tree trunks close to the ground, and the southern bracket fungus, which is thick, semi-circular and can reach up to 2 feet across.

Shady plants edge the path through Pithill Wood: wood sorrel, foxgloves and the wonderfully named enchanter's nightshade, which has tiny white flowers and large oval-shaped leaves.

Look out for patches of navelwort on the moss-covered walls of the Kings Gutter, and for tangles of honeysuckle and wild clematis along the lane at the end of the walk.

Honey fungus

4 ▬ Keep **left** at the junction to cut across a bend in the river.
▬ Walk to the next path junction in 125 yards.

5 ▬ Turn **left** up a narrow and steeply ascending path; keep **straight on** where a narrower path heads off left downhill, and continue to a path T-junction.

6 ▬ Turn **left** to cross a low wall, now on the Kings Gutter path.
▬ This continues for just under ½ mile to a path-end barrier.

78 Short Walks Made Easy

Publishing information

© Crown copyright 2024.
All rights reserved.

Ordnance Survey, OS, and the OS logos are registered trademarks, and OS Short Walks Made Easy is a trademark of Ordnance Survey Ltd.

© Crown copyright and database rights (2023) Ordnance Survey.

ISBN 978 0 319092 73 6
1st edition published by Ordnance Survey 2024.

www.ordnancesurvey.co.uk

While every care has been taken to ensure the accuracy of the route directions, the publishers cannot accept responsibility for errors or omissions, or for changes in details given. The countryside is not static: hedges and fences can be removed, stiles can be replaced by gates, field boundaries can alter, footpaths can be rerouted and changes in ownership can result in the closure or diversion of some concessionary paths. Also, paths that are easy and pleasant for walking in fine conditions may become slippery, muddy and difficult in wet weather.

If you find an inaccuracy in either the text or maps, please contact Ordnance Survey at os.uk/contact.

All rights reserved. No part of this publication may be reproduced, transmitted in any form or by any means, or stored in a retrieval system without either the prior written permission of the publisher, or in the case of reprographic reproduction a licence issued in accordance with the terms and licences issued by the CLA Ltd.

A catalogue record for this book is available from the British Library.

Milestone Publishing credits

Author: Sue Viccars

Series editor: Kevin Freeborn

Maps: Cosmographics

Design and Production: Patrick Dawson, Milestone Publishing

Printed in India by Replika Press Pvt. Ltd

Photography credits

Front cover: ClimbWhenReady/Shutterstock.com.
Back cover cornfield/Shutterstock.com.

All photographs supplied by the author ©Sue Viccars except page 6 Tom Sigler (Ordnance Survey); page 39 Kevin Freeborn.

The following images were supplied by Shutterstock.com: page 7 Jonathan Hicks; 9 Jasper Suijten; 19 Christian Musat; 19 Edwin Godinho; 33, 66, 73 Erni; 33 HWall; 33 Marek Mierzejewski; 38 Dick Kenny; 40 Dennis Jacobsen; 40 Zeno Swijtink; 41 Liz Miller; 41 Matthias Brix; 47 ArvydasS; 47 Monika Surzin; 47 Tiuku Laakso; 59 Alex Coope; 59 Stephen Farhall; 67 John Griffiths; 72 Ivan Marjanovic; 73 Ian W Douglas; 79 Ihor Hvozdetskyi.

Top left: navelwort
Top right: foxglove
Above: grey squirrel
Left: dipper

P a t h — Path-end barrier — 1½ miles — The arrival of the railway ☆ — Station Road (roadside parking) 🅿

7 ▶ Beyond the barrier, reach a lane. ▶ Turn **left** and then follow the lane **downhill** to pass under the viaduct back to the start.

Local legend The Erme is said to be haunted by Treneman, a man who drowned in the river, was hauled out and hung upside down in an abortive attempt to drain the water out of him. This action eroded a basin in the rock below, and 'Treneman's Basin' and 'Treneman's Pool' live on to this day. Stand by the rock at midnight, call out 'More rope!' and his ghost will appear and chase you through the woods...

Walk 10 Longtimber Woods